Note from the authors

As an adult, we wouldn't go to a job interview without some preparation and it's the same for children and their 11+ interviews! This book is written for the children to work through themselves. It includes a clear guide and workbook to help children prepare for 11+ interviews and aids parents in supporting their child through the process with advice and guidance.

11+ Interview Practice Skills

Please direct all enquiries to the authors.

Printed in the United Kingdom.

Publisher: Independent Publishing Network
Publication date: August 2023
ISBN: 978-1-80352-826-7
Authors: Charlotte Badenoch and Danielle Okumura

www.brightlighteducation.co.uk

CONTENTS

Welcome!

Welcome to our 11+ Interview Practice Skills book. First of all, well done for working so hard during primary school. It will soon to be time to go to the next stage of your academic journey! If you have been preparing for the 11+ examinations already, we hope your studies are going well and you are gradually gaining in confidence in all the different areas.

We have created this book not as an extra chore for you, but as a tool to give you a greater understanding of the 11+ interview process. We really hope you enjoy working through it and that you reach the end of the book with interview skill superpowers!

The book also includes an essential section on developing a growth mindset. Your friends and family know you are a wonderfully positive and resilient person, but how will you get this across to the interviewer? We hope you enjoy working through our activities to help bring out that truly fabulous personality.

Summary

WHAT?	The interviews are an opportunity for the prospective school to get to know you, your interests and hobbies as well as your enthusiasm for learning.
PREPARATION	Preparation for interviews is not to learn all your answers off by heart! It is about building confidence in what you will be discussing with the interviewer.
MOCKS	Mock interviews are a great way to practice and ensure you are not feeling too nervous before the actual interview.
1:1 / GROUP	The majority of interviews will be on a 1:1 basis, but occasionally schools will interview children in groups.
ONLINE	Online interviews do still happen. They typically follow a similar pattern to face-to-face interviews.

What are the 11+ Interviews?

11+ interviews are often used as part of the admissions process for independent schools in the UK. These interviews are typically used to assess a student's potential and suitability for the school. The school has to be right for the child and the child has to have the potential to thrive at the school.

Generally, interviews are after the examination and, whilst some schools only choose children who have passed the examination, other schools will interview all candidates irrespective of whether they have passed the examination.

Many schools use a three-stage process. There is an examination, a reference is sent from the child's current school and then the interview is usually the final stage. In short, the interview is a chance for the school to get an idea of the child's personality to see whether they are a good fit for the school.

Schools largely interview between 8-10 children for each place available so that means there is a lot riding on the interview! It is a perfect opportunity for you to stand out from the rest. They are not used to scare you and, in general, they just want to get to know you, your interests and hobbies, and get a sense of your enthusiasm for learning.

Do I need to prepare?

Many schools state that children do not need to prepare for an interview. We would suggest this is partly true in that there is nothing worse than a child answering an interview question with a rote-learned answer! However, an adult wouldn't go to a job interview without preparation so it's the same for children! It is obviously not about learning answers by rote, but preparation can be hugely beneficial to give you that fighting chance to succeed. This guide and workbook allows you to do just that.

Sometimes, schools request that each child brings something to the interview to talk about; it could be something you have created or something which is important to you. Some schools ask each child to give a short presentation on a topic of their choice. In these circumstances, you will of course need to prepare something in advance.

Should I have a mock Interview?

Mock Interviews can be helpful for you as they give you a little practice before the real thing. Bright Light Education offer mock interviews to help prepare children for their interviews, which include detailed feedback on how the mock interview went. You can also practise at home, and, at the end of this book, we have some example mock interviews that you might like to use.

What will the interview be like?

1:1 Interviews

The majority of interviews are on a one-to-one basis and you will be interviewed by either the Head teacher, the Deputy Head Teacher or a Head of Department/age range. These generally last around 20 minutes.

Occasionally there might be more than one interviewer, so make sure you are not put off if this is the case! Ensure you speak to and make eye contact with both or all of the interviewers.

Group Interviews

There are many schools that choose to use a group interview. The schools are looking for how you interact with the other children, how you position yourself within the group and how you problem solve as a team. The school is not expecting every child to be the one who takes the lead within the group and neither will they only choose that confident, extroverted child. They look at those children who do not perhaps take the main role within the group to see how they interact and negotiate as a part of a team despite not taking control! It is important that you get involved within the dynamic of the group and contribute to the task, challenge or discussion points.

It is also vital to show that you can listen, speak to the other children and take on board others' points and ideas. Often schools will provide a challenge or a task to see how you respond.

Online Interviews

Interviews may be conducted online. They typically follow a similar pattern to face-to-face interviews. It's still important for you to present yourself well. Make sure you have a quiet room; the webcam is set up properly and the sound is set up well. Ensure you are ready and prepared before logging in to the interview. The questions are likely to be very similar to an in-person interview.

Good luck! Remember that no interview is the same and there are no set rules for what might happen in the interview. Try to enjoy yourself and let us know how you get on.

Research

What do I know about the interviews?

All schools differ so it's worthwhile finding out from the school itself any details they are willing to give out regarding the interview process. This will help you prepare for what is to come.

Task: Make notes on your research for each of your potential school interviews.

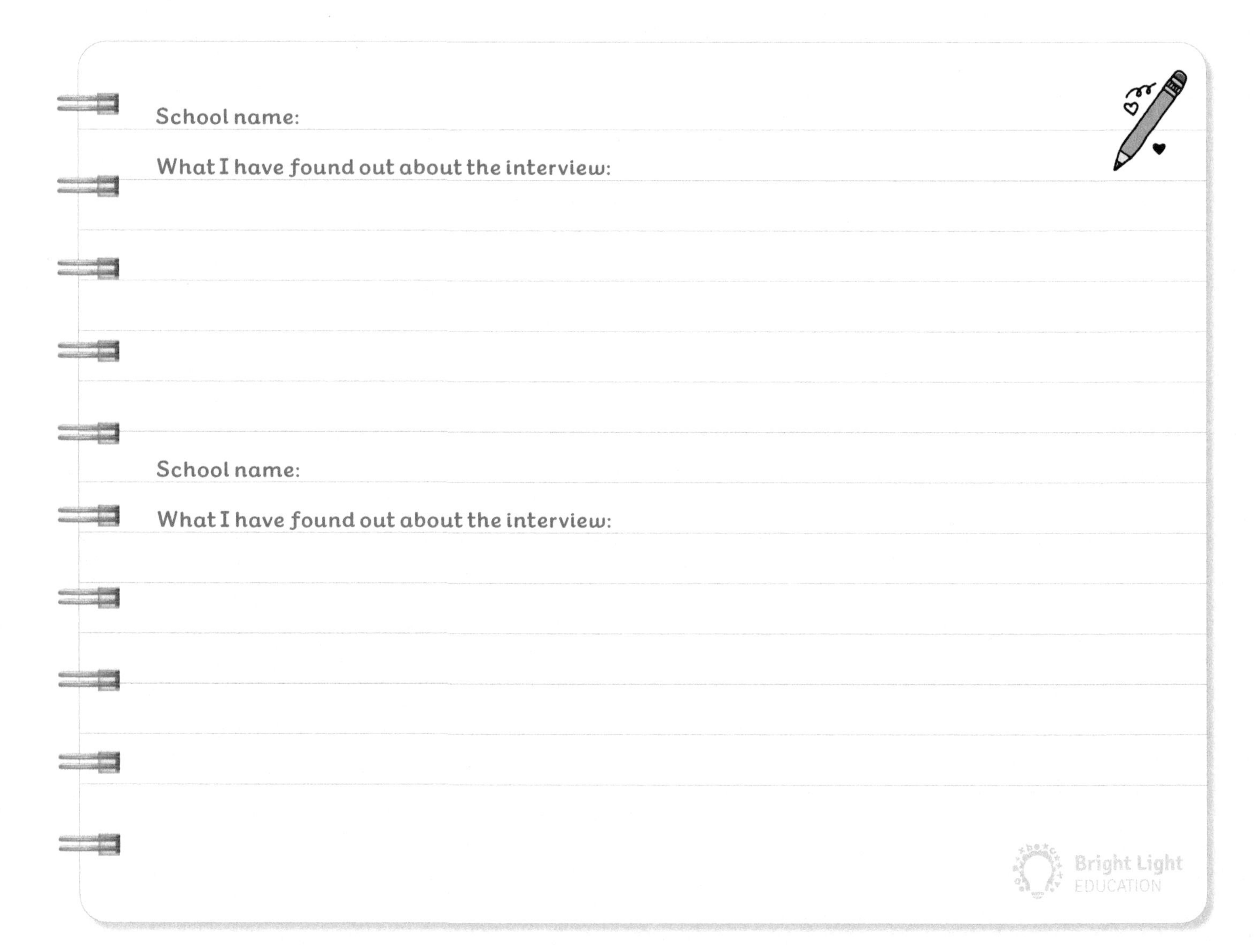

School name:

What I have found out about the interview:

School name:

What I have found out about the interview:

School name:

What I have found out about the interview:

SCHOOL

Bright Light EDUCATION

Research

What are schools looking for?

If you were the interviewer, what would you look for in a candidate to your school?

Task: Write down 5 things you think are important.

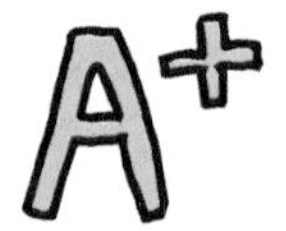

Now take a look at what schools are looking for

Did you have any of the same points? Schools look for a variety of qualities.

These may include:

Academic ability: Schools will often assess a child's potential suitability for the school by looking at academic ability. This could include academic achievements as well as test results.

Intellectual curiosity: Schools will be looking for children who are curious and eager to learn. This might include asking you about your interests and hobbies, as well as your knowledge of current events and other topics.

Communication skills: Schools will look at a child's communication skills by asking questions and observing how you respond. This might include your ability to express yourself clearly and listen attentively.

Confidence: Schools might be looking for students who are confident and capable of expressing themselves. This might include asking you about your interests and hobbies, as well as observing your body language and demeanour.

Motivation and determination: Schools look for children who are motivated and determined to succeed. This might include asking you about your goals and aspirations, as well as your dedication to your studies and extracurricular activities.

Social skills: Schools will be looking at your social skills by observing your interactions with others, including the interviewer and other candidates. This might include your ability to work in a group, showing empathy and making friends.

Creativity and problem-solving skills: Schools like to look for students who are able to think creatively and solve problems. This might include asking you to solve problems or puzzles, or to think on your feet during the interview.

Special Talents: Schools look for whether children have particular talents which the school might be able to develop within the school.

Overall fit: Schools may also consider whether a student is a good fit for their school culture and community. This might include looking at your interests, personality and values.

What do I know about the schools?

Familiarise yourself with the school's mission and values. You can usually find this information on the school's website.

Task: Use this page to write down bullet point notes on any schools you have interviews for.

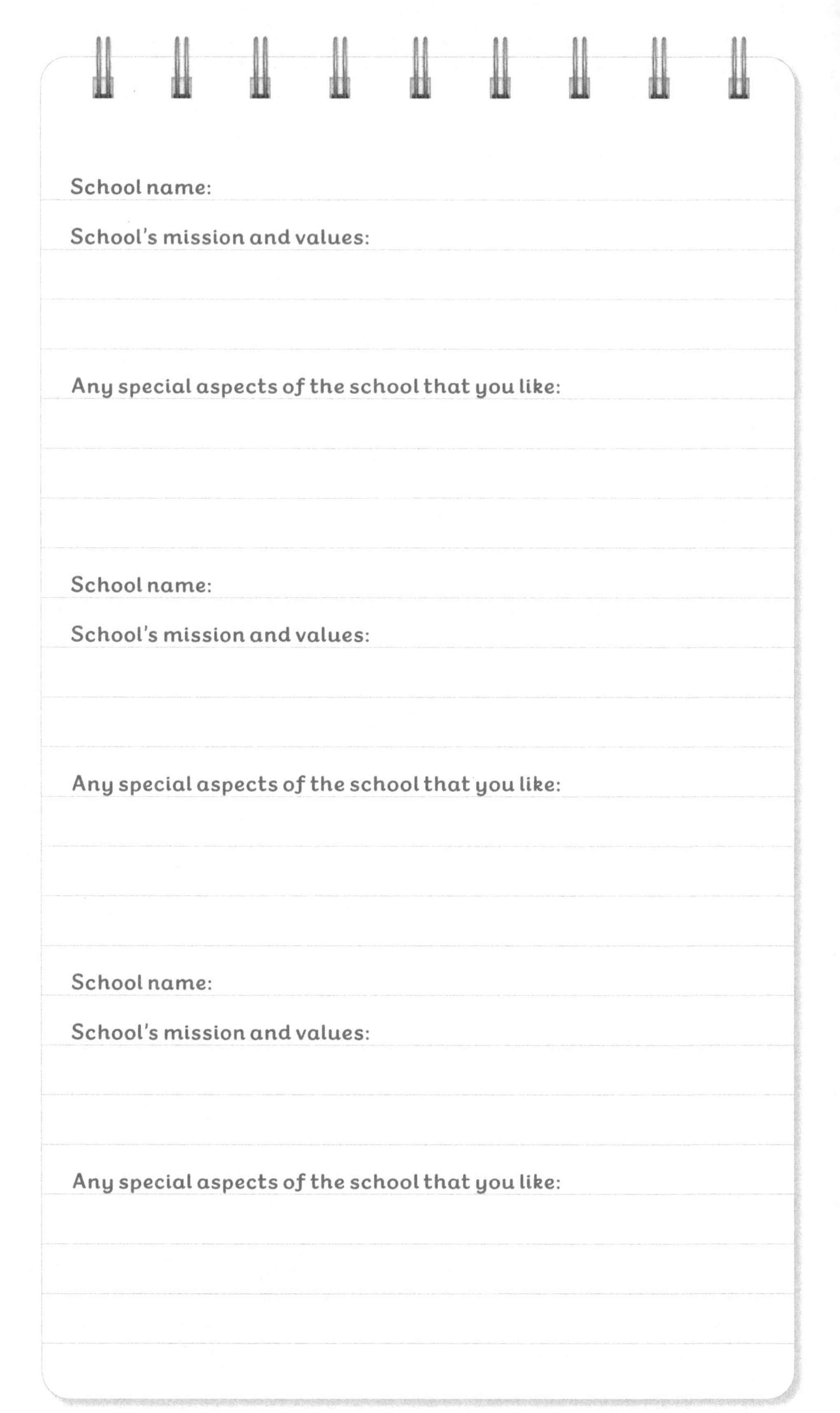

What have I learned from previous interviews?

Use this page to jot down any interview questions you can remember as they may come up again in your next interview!

Task: Can you jot down some notes as to how you might answer them?

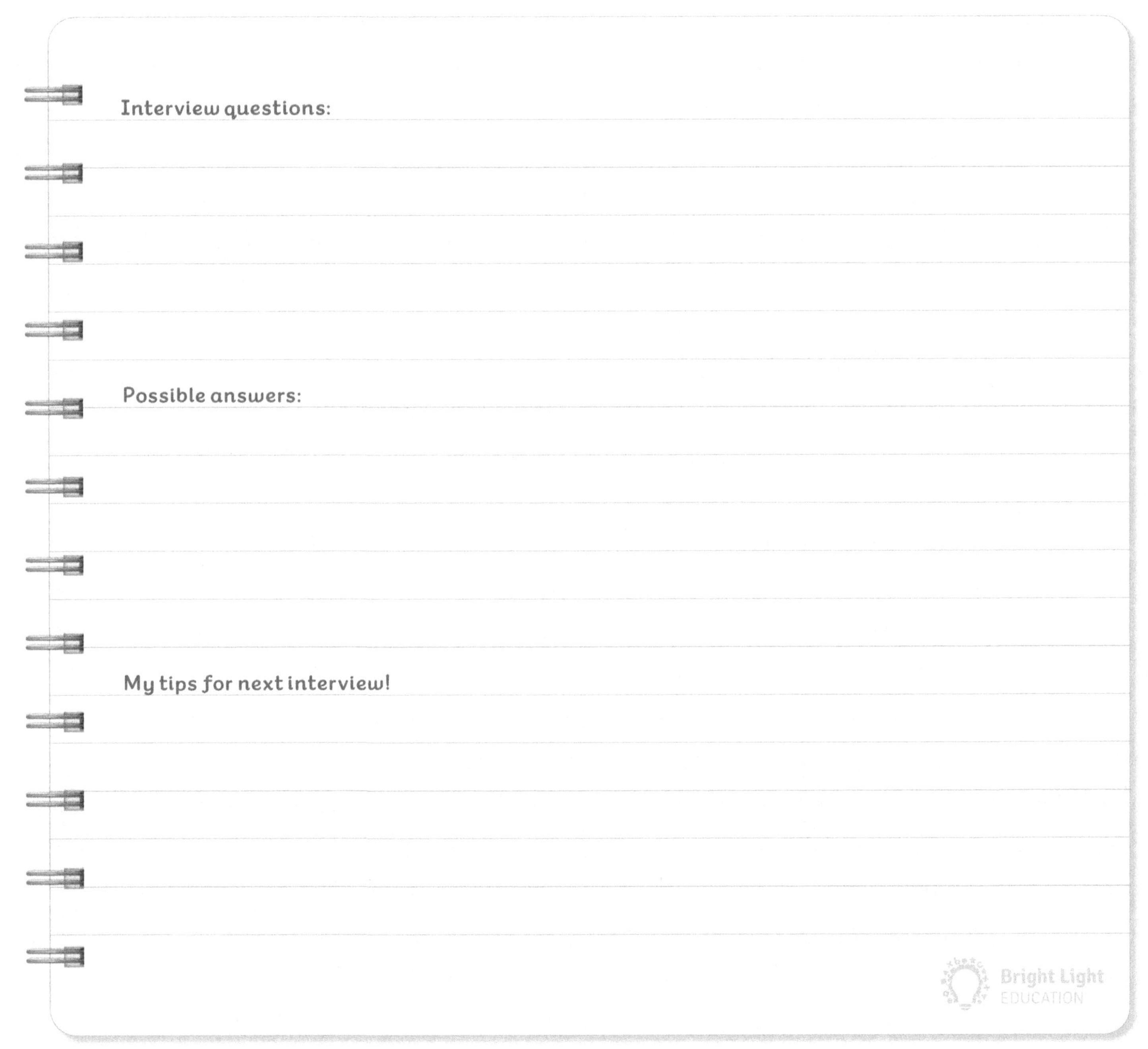

Growth Mindset

What is a growth mindset?

A growth mindset is the belief that one's abilities and intelligence can be developed through effort and learning.

This mindset encourages resilience, a love of learning, and a willingness to take on new challenges, leading to personal and intellectual growth. Schools want students who have a growth mindset because it fosters a positive and productive learning environment.

Look at the growth mindset questions below.
Task: Can you think of personal examples which you could share in an interview in response to the questions? Jot down your thoughts.

Growth mindset questions	Your thoughts
Embrace challenges • Do you seek out new challenges and view them as opportunities for growth rather than obstacles?	
Learn from feedback • Do you use feedback as a tool to improve, rather than getting defensive or taking it personally?	
Try new things • Do you step out of your comfort zone and try new activities, even if there is a risk of failure? • Do you attempt to take on new learning opportunities like new hobbies, sports, or clubs, to continue to develop your abilities and intelligence?	
Persist in the face of setbacks • Do you keep working towards goals and don't give up easily?	

Growth mindset questions	Your thoughts
Surround yourself with positive people • Do you surround yourself with people who have a growth mindset and who will support and encourage personal growth?	
Reflect on your own mindset • Do you reflect on your own thoughts and beliefs about learning and growth and make a conscious effort to change a fixed mindset to growth mindset?	
Goal setting • Do you set and work towards specific goals, such as learning a new skill or completing a project? • Do you try breaking big goals down into smaller, more manageable tasks?	
Failure celebration • Do you celebrate your failures and see them as opportunities to learn and grow? • Do you understand that failure is a natural part of the learning process?	
Mindset reflection • Do you reflect on your own thoughts and beliefs about learning and growth? • Do you challenge those negative thoughts and replace them with positive ones?	
Mindful learning • Do you try and be present in the moment and focus on the task at hand? • Do you stay motivated and engaged in the learning process?	

How can I develop my growth mindset?

Having a growth mindset does not always come easily! It's natural to feel pessimistic, frustrated or disappointed at times. Here are a few activities you can do to help develop your growth mindset, which should then help you to feel more positive when going into your interview.

Put a positive spin on it!

Negative
Look at the worry below:

Positive
Now look at the positive spin I can put on my worry:

I know that with practice and patience, I can become a better reader. Every time I read, I'm learning new words and stories that help my imagination grow. I ask for help from my teacher, parents, and friends, and they show me fun ways to practise reading. It's okay to make mistakes because that's how I learn and get better!

Read these three worries below and change the language to put a positive spin on them.

Now write one of your own, perhaps choosing an example which might reflect one of your own worries.

How about you share your worry with a family member and see how they can help you put a positive spin on it?

Failure to Success!

It is important to remind yourself that failing at something is not the end of the world. Do you know any famous people who failed first before becoming a success?

Sometimes you will face certain difficulties and you might feel like you haven't succeeded in something.

For these things, ask yourself the following questions:

- What happened?
- What was the result?
- How did you feel at the time?
- What have you learned that can help?
- What will you do next time?
- How will you motivate yourself to succeed next time?

"Failure is simply the opportunity to begin again, this time more intelligently."

Henry Ford Founder of the Ford Motor Company

"I've missed more than 9000 shots in my career. I've lost almost 300 games. 26 times, I've been trusted to take the game winning shot and missed. I've failed over and over and over again in my life. And that is why I succeed."

Michael Jordan
One of the greatest basketball players of all time

"I was the biggest failure I knew and as poor as one can be in England without having to be homeless."

JK Rowling
Author of Harry Potter

Research the two famous people here. Try to find out how they turned their failures into successes!

For the last example, write about yourself. Think of a time when you have turned a failure into a success and write about what happened.

Ludwig van Beethoven

SUCCESS

Serena Williams

About me

Happiness Journal

Despite our best intentions, it's sometimes difficult to focus on the good things that happened in your day, rather than focussing on the thing that brought you down.

Feeling positive is important for your growth mindset, as well as helping the growth mindset of others! In an interview, you want to send a positive energy across to your interviewer!

Next week, create a Happiness Journal, in which you write down each day anything that happened which brought a smile to your face. Can you also think of times when you brought a smile to someone else's face? Jot down those special moments too!

Happiness Journal

Week of ______________________

MONDAY	FRIDAY
TUESDAY	SATURDAY
WEDNESDAY	SUNDAY
THURSDAY	NOTES

Confidence Boosting

It's time for you to have a big confidence boost! Your friends and family know you are amazing, but do you know you are?! Being able to recognise the sensational things about yourself is important, not only for your interview, but for developing self-confidence and a healthy mental well-being.

Think of all the amazing people that you know in the world. Why are they amazing? These can be people you know (family, friends, teachers, other adults and children) as well as famous people.

Now think about why you are amazing! In the picture frame below, write down all the great things about you. You might even like to stick a copy on your door or mirror to remind yourself every morning!

Forming an opinion

For some of us, sharing our opinions comes easily but for others, a wave of self-consciousness can overpower the ability to put forward a personal thought or idea. Here are a couple of ways to practise forming your own opinion.

What's Better?
Work through the topics below with a friend or family member to debate what's better. Remember every opinion is valid! Try to give a reason for your answer.

Add your own three ideas in the last boxes!

Cats or Dogs?	Rich and famous or Rich and unknown?	Phone or No phone?
Pineapple pizza or Apple pasta?	Talking pets or Talking babies?	Bad haircut or Bad hair dye?
Working hard or Hardly working?	Silly hats or Silly socks?	Winter or Summer?
Mountains or Oceans?	Art museum or History museum?	Being embarrassed or Being afraid?
Plans or Surprises?	Animals or People?	Poems or Stories?
Success or Happiness?	Student or Teacher?	Sun or Moon?
or	or	or

Dinner Table Discussions

Breakfast and dinner time discussions with your family are a great way to build up your confidence when having conversations.

Task: Photocopy and cut out these discussion topics and leave them on your dinner table for a post-dinner debate!

What's one skill you wish you had?

What would the title of your autobiography be?

If you could time travel, would you go to the past or the future and why?

What's something new you want to try this year?

Talk about your favourite place for one minute.

If you could become invisible for the day, what would you do?

Dinner Table Discussions

Task: Photocopy and cut out these discussion topics and leave them on your dinner table for a post-dinner debate!

Tell us something nice you did for someone today.	**Name one thing you are looking forward to.**
Where would you fly to if you had wings?	**Can you feel happy and sad at the same time?**
Name something that someone else at the table is good at.	**What is the hardest thing about being a child?**

What advice would you ask your future self?

What is one thing you learned today that you found interesting?

What are two goals you would like to achieve over the next year?

Is it better to read a book or watch a movie?

What are you most thankful for today?

Have you become 'you' yet?

Personal interests and achievements

What are my interests?

If you have worked through the previous chapter, you should now be developing your growth mindset and hopefully feeling more and more positive about how incredibly fabulous you are.

It's time to move on to personal interests and specific achievements. The interviewer may ask you about your hobbies and extracurricular activities, as well as any awards or recognition you have received. You might need to look back at certificates and awards so that you can remember your past achievements.

Think about the following:

Look at our example pin board and then, on the following page, choose from the headings above to create your own pin board.

EXAMPLE PIN BOARD

All about me

LANGUAGES

- Attend the French lunchtime club at school.
- Speak Spanish at home.

MUSIC

Play the flute – grade 4.
Attend school choir.

ROLES AT SCHOOL

I was part of the school council in Year 5 and we had half termly meetings with the deputy head teacher to discuss how to improve our school.

In Year 4, I was part of the 'green team' which met to discuss how we could make our school more eco-friendly.

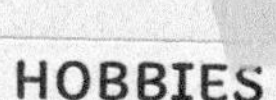

HOBBIES

I like skateboarding and have recently bought my first skateboard with money I earned.

REUSE ME

READING

Current book:
The Boy at the Back of the Class.

Want to read:
Matilda as I've never read it!

Personal interests and achievements

Create your own pin board. Try to add detail! Keep adding to your pin board over the next couple of weeks and read it over several times, especially just before your interview.

What books do I enjoy?

You may be asked a question about the book you are reading or books you have read and enjoyed.

Task: Use these book templates to jot down books that you have read recently to help you remember them before your interview.

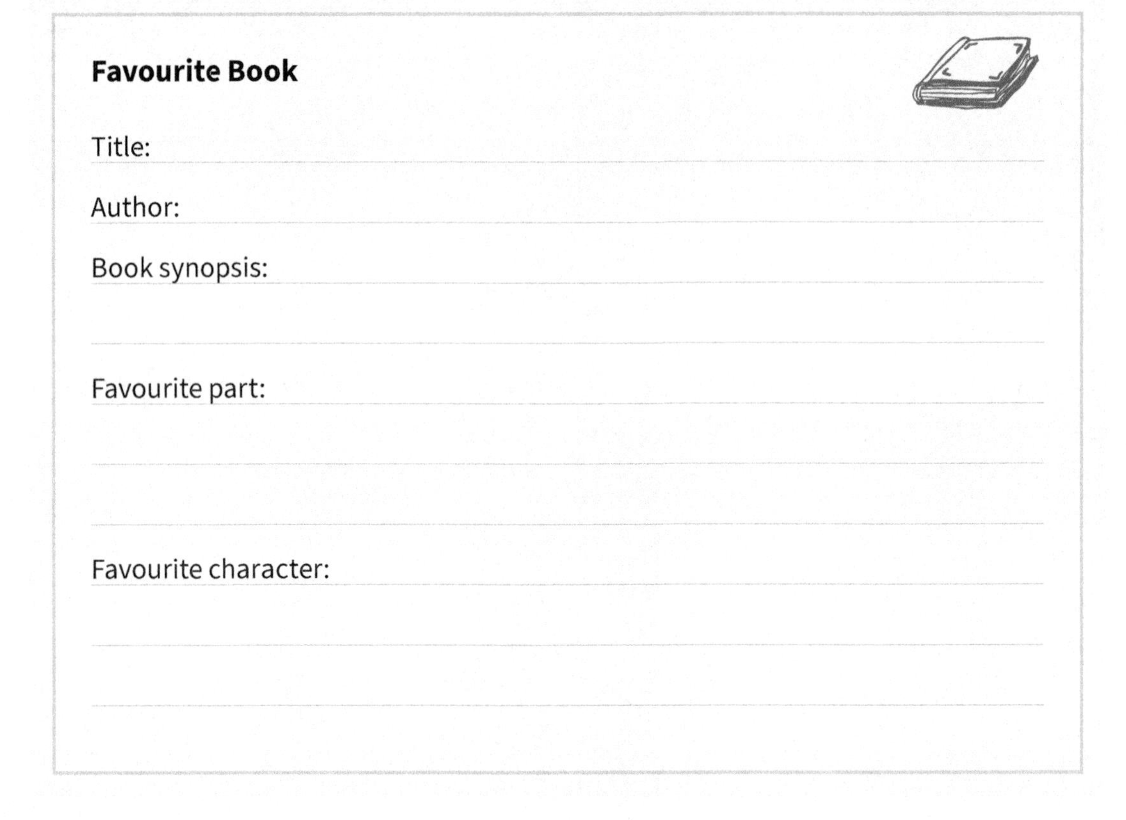

Favourite Book

Title:

Author:

Book synopsis:

Favourite part:

Favourite character:

Favourite Book

READING

Title:

Author:

Book synopsis:

Favourite part:

Favourite character:

Favourite Book

Title:

Author:

Book synopsis:

Favourite part:

Favourite character:

Favourite Book

Title:

Author:

Book synopsis:

Favourite part:

Favourite character:

The interview

What are some top tips for the interview?

You're developing your growth mindset, building that confidence and lastly, reminding yourself of all your interests and achievements. You're ready to start thinking about the interview itself! Research shows that first impressions are made within 7 seconds of meeting someone. How will you make your first impression a good one?!

What should I wear?

- You want to be neat and smart but comfortable. Don't wear something that you've never worn before as you'll be distracted by a new button or an uncomfortable zip! Wear something that makes you feel good!
- Don't wear anything too informal – avoid tracksuit bottoms!
- One good option is to wear your school uniform. It is something you are familiar with, it's not out of character and it fits well.

How should I behave?

Be polite: Don't forget to greet your interviewer at the start and say 'Thank you' at the end.

Sit properly: Think about your posture and keep your back straight. Don't slouch or lean on the table. Try not to fidget.

Smile: Smiling releases endorphins and can help you feel less nervous. Smiling is also contagious and so you can help to put your interviewer into a better mood through your smiles!

Be you: The interviewer is trying to get to know you, so don't be afraid to let your beautiful personality shine through.

What will I wear?

Draw yourself here in the interview

How should I answer the questions?

Feel proud and enthusiastic: Using what you have learned in this book, feel confident about all the wonderful things about you.

Be natural: Don't memorise answers – it will be obvious if you do and will sound unnatural. Talk from the heart.

Be curious and show interest: Stay focussed and make eye contact with your interviewer. Listen to the questions carefully! If you are in a group interview, make sure you show interest in what other people are saying.

Give examples: Try to expand on your answers by giving further details on the topic. Don't make your answer too short. Or too long! Try to avoid repeating yourself.

Take your time: A short pause whilst you gather your thoughts before answering a question is fine.

Don't panic: If you're stuck on how to answer the question, it's ok to say something like, "That's an interesting question and something I've never thought about before." It's also fine to ask the interviewer to clarify the question.

*And please... **Avoid saying** ...and stuff.*

Sample interview questions

We will now look at sample interview questions for you to have a go at answering. We have divided the questions into different types of question.

Task: Have a go at answering these questions on the lines provided. Remember, you don't want to learn answers off by heart, so you might choose to write notes rather than full sentences.

About you and your family

1. What activities do you like to do with your family?

   - Watch movies on a Friday night
   - Taking turns choosing

   2. Hikes

2. Tell me about a book you have read.

   "How do you live"

   - Why did you like it?
   - What would you change about it?

3. Tell me about a real interest you have, either in or out of school.

   - Violin

4. What is your greatest strength?

   Humor

5. What three words would you use to describe yourself?

   Easy-going, humorous, empathetic.

~~who~~ who is your favorite musician

Oslo Opera House

6. What do you want to be when you grow up?

Computer programmer or architect. → Falling Waters

7. If you had 2 hours of free time, what would you do?

read, comic books, video games.

8. Tell me about something you found difficult and what happened.

9. Who is your favourite sportsperson, musician or artist?

Magritte – Museum in Brussels because my dad is Belgian.

10. If you could be anyone for a day, who would you be?

11. Can you think of any other questions about you and your family that you might be asked?

Tell me of something you would like to get better at

About you and your school

1. What is your favourite subject and why?

Literacy (reading & writing)

2. What is your least favourite subject and why?

3. What would your teachers say about you if I asked them?

4. What extra-curricular activities do you do?

Judo
Swimming
Skiing

Violin

5. Tell me about a piece of group work or teamwork you were involved in.

6. What would your dream school be like?

7. Do you have a school responsibility? If so, what have you learned from this role?

8. What would you change about your school?

9. Can you think of any other questions about you and your school that you might be asked?

Do you have any questions about this school?

About this school

1. What attracts you to our school?

2. What will you contribute to this school?

3. Is there anything about this school which would be challenging for you?

4. Which other schools have you applied for? Which one is your favourite?

5. Can you think of any other questions about this school that you might be asked?

Complex ideas

These questions are not used to catch you out, but are merely a good way of the interviewer getting to know you a little better and introducing some possible discussion topics. They want to hear your thinking and reasoning. There are no right answers here, but be sure to continue to show enthusiasm and interest in what you are being asked.

1. What makes a good teacher?

2. What makes a good pupil?

3. If you could have any job for a day, what would it be and why?

4. If you were given £300, what would you do with it and why?

5. If you were a superhero, what would your superpower be?

6. If you could solve one problem in the world, what would it be and why?

Sample interview questions

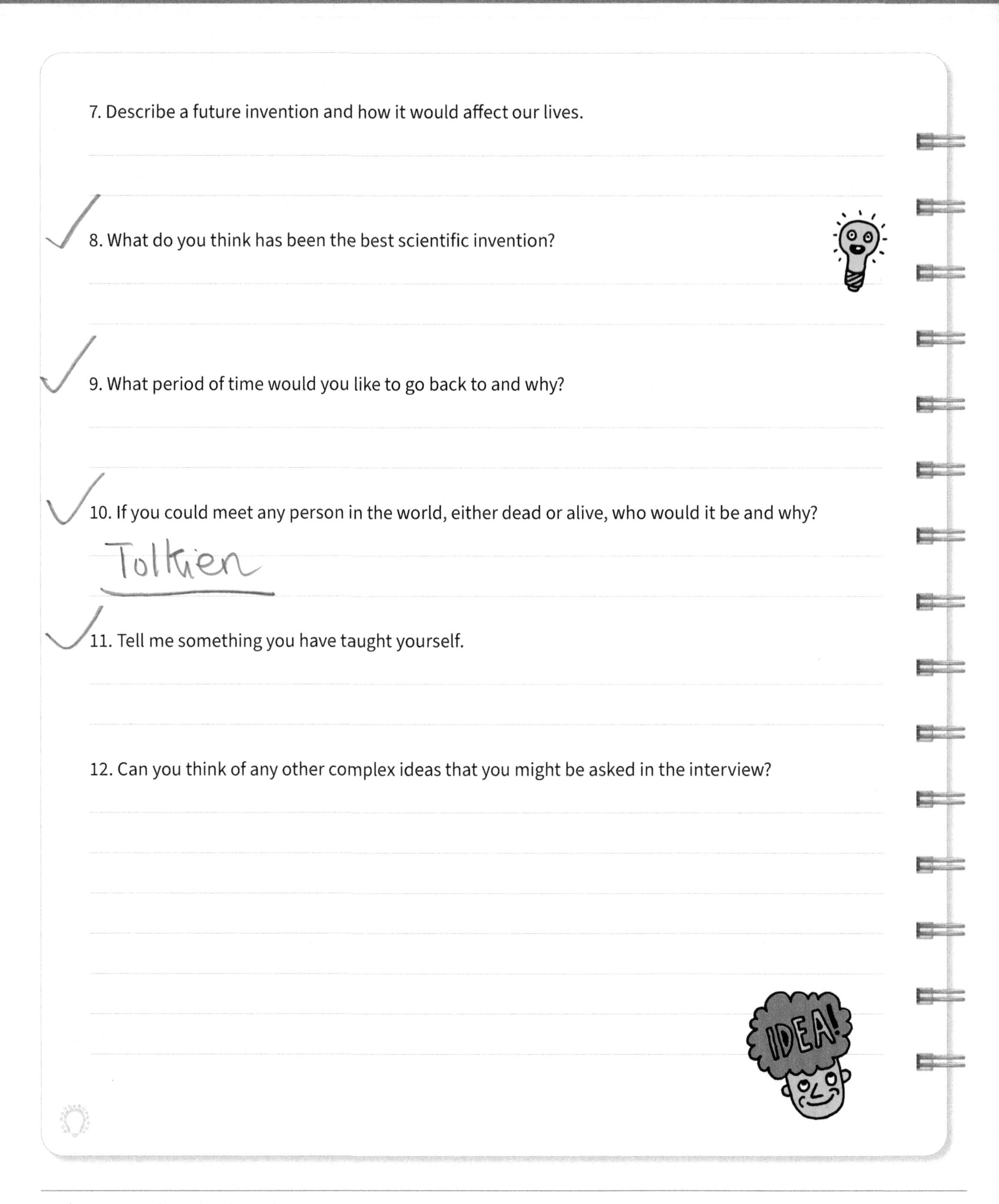

7. Describe a future invention and how it would affect our lives.

8. What do you think has been the best scientific invention?

9. What period of time would you like to go back to and why?

10. If you could meet any person in the world, either dead or alive, who would it be and why?

Tolkien

11. Tell me something you have taught yourself.

12. Can you think of any other complex ideas that you might be asked in the interview?

Unusual questions

Some questions you just cannot predict and you must really think creatively about your answer! There is no right or wrong answer to these questions and interviewers are wanting to see how you think on your feet! These are tricky (if not impossible) questions to prepare for, but it is useful to see examples of the types of unusual questions that could arise. Thinking of your own unusual questions can be a fun way to bring about discussions with friends or family and this will ensure you aren't too surprised if one comes up in your actual interview!

1. Think of as many things as possible that you could do with a pen other than use it as a pen.

2. This watch doesn't have batteries. How do the hands move?

3. What would you do with a brick?

Sample interview questions

4. If you were given the ability to talk to animals for one day, how would you use this unique opportunity?

5. How many ice-cubes would fill this room?

6. How does a radio work?

7. Tell me about this banana.

8. Can you think of any other unusual questions that you might be asked in the interview?

Higher order questions

Higher order questions, sometimes referred to as debate questions or moral questions are those that require some analysis and thoughts to both sides of the argument. Ideally you would come to a logical conclusion.

1. How should we be supporting people who have no home?

2. Is there more happiness or unhappiness in the world?

3. What colour would a zebra be if it lost all its stripes?

4. Is it possible to have a box with nothing inside?

5. Should billions of pounds be spent on space exploration when there is poverty in the world?

Sample interview questions

6. Should we all become vegan to reduce carbon emissions and habitat destruction caused by meat production?

7. The police want greater access to the public's personal data (e.g. internet search history, encrypted phone messages). What's more important, your right to personal privacy or public safety?

8. The voting age in England is 18 (in general elections), but there are discussions about changing it. What do you think the voting age should be and why?

9. Can you think of any other higher order questions that you might be asked an interview?

Mental maths questions

Sometimes you will be asked maths questions. Generally you will be required to work these out mentally rather than using a paper and pencil.

1. If a car travels 100 miles in 2 hours, what is its average speed per hour?

2. What is a third of three quarters of 1000?

3. How many faces does a hexagonal based prism have?

4. What is 20% of 600?

5. What is the percentage increase from 20 to 30?

6. A rectangle has a length of 18 cm and a width of 9 cm.
What is the area of the rectangle?

7. A store sells 25 bags of rice each day. If each bag contains 2.5 kg of rice, how many kg of rice are sold in one week (7 days)?

8. Calculate 2896 + 384

9. Work out 241 ÷ 25

10. Which two numbers have a sum of 15 and a product of 36?

Top Tip: Don't rush these – you are not being timed! Take your time and work through the question, saying it aloud before explaining how you will work it out if you don't know the answer immediately.

Describing an image

In some interviews, you might be asked to discuss an image. You might be given specific questions regarding the image or you might simply be asked to talk about it. Again, there is no right or wrong answer to these questions. Interviewers are looking for enlightening and interesting responses!

It is difficult to prepare for this type of question. The best thing to do is to look at different images and have discussions around them with a friend or adult. Ask questions, however unusual they might be, and see where the discussion takes you!

If you are given an image and asked simply to talk about it, there are a few questions you might like to consider:

- What media is it? i.e. Is it a photograph/ painting?
- How would you describe it?
- What do you think its purpose is?
- How does it make you feel?
- Does it remind you of another image you have seen before?
- How do you think the artist felt when they created it?

Task: Look at the two images and jot down your ideas, using the questions above to guide you.

Image 1

Image 2

Image: 1. Nighthawks (1942) by Edward Hopper **2.** The Starry Night (1889) by Vincent van Gogh

Responding to questions about an image

Sometimes you might be shown an image and asked various questions about it.

Task: Look at the following images and write down answers to the questions that follow.

Image 1

1. What can you see in this image?

2. Can you identify any objects in this image?

3. How do you think this image was created?

4. What does this image make you think of?

Image 2

1. What do you like about this image?

2. What do you think is happening in this image?

3. How do you think the person in this image is feeling?

4. Why do you think this photo was taken?

Image: 1. White Zig-Zags (1922) by Wassily Kandinsky **2.** Martin Luther King by Wiki Images

Discussing a passage

You may be asked to read a passage of prose in an interview and be asked questions relating to that passage. This is very similar to comprehension questions, only you are answering the questions orally.

Obviously, you don't know what passage will come up in an interview, but practising comprehension questions verbally with an adult and discussing a piece of text is a perfect way to practise this type of question. Many of these answers will be subjective.

Task: Read the passage and answer the questions that follow.

Sophie was always fascinated by space and the possibility of extra-terrestrial life. She spent countless hours studying stars and planets, and dreaming of one day becoming an astronaut. One day, while gazing through her telescope, she spotted a strange object moving across the sky. At first, she thought it might be a shooting star, but then she realized it was moving too slowly and changing direction. Sophie's heart raced as she realised that she might have just discovered something truly amazing.

Interview questions:

1. What is Sophie fascinated by?

2. What did Sophie spot while she was gazing through her telescope?

3. How did Sophie feel when she realised that she might have discovered something truly amazing?

4. If you had the opportunity to explore space, what planet or star would you want to visit and why?

5. What do you think is the most important quality for an astronaut to have?

6. How do you think the discovery of extra-terrestrial life would impact our world?

7. Have you ever seen a shooting star? If so, what was it like?

8. Do you think it's important for humans to explore space? Why or why not?

9. What kind of training do you think astronauts have to go through before they can go to space?

10. What do you think is the most challenging part of being an astronaut?

Discussing a poem

You may be asked to read a poem and discuss it with the interviewer.

Task: Read the poem below and answer the questions that follow.

My Shadow

I have a little shadow that goes in and out with me,
And what can be the use of him is more than I can see.
He is very, very like me from the heels up to the head;
And I see him jump before me, when I jump into my bed.
The funniest thing about him is the way he likes to grow–
Not at all like proper children, which is always very slow;
For he sometimes shoots up taller like an india-rubber ball,
And he sometimes gets so little that there's none of him at all.

He hasn't got a notion of how children ought to play,
And can only make a fool of me in every sort of way.
He stays so close beside me, he's a coward you can see;
I'd think shame to stick to nursie as that shadow sticks to me!

One morning, very early, before the sun was up,
I rose and found the shining dew on every buttercup;
But my lazy little shadow, like an arrant sleepy-head,
Had stayed at home behind me and was fast asleep in bed.

Robert Louis Stevenson

Questions:

1. What is the poem 'My Shadow' about?

2. How would you describe the relationship between the speaker and their shadow?

3. Why do you think the speaker is so interested in their shadow?

4. What does the speaker mean when they say,
"And sometimes, when the sun is low, I see a face I know?"

5. Have you ever played with your shadow? What did you do?

6. Do you think shadows have feelings? Why or why not?

7. What do you think the poem tells us about the nature of light and shadows?

8. How might you feel if your shadow could talk to you?

9. What is your favourite line or phrase from the poem, and why?

10. How does the poem make you feel?

Current affairs and topical issues

A common question in interviews is asking you about current affairs and topical issues. It is vital you keep on top of what is happening in the world around you and be prepared to discuss these with the interviewer.

Current affairs resources:
There are many ways to keep up to date with current affairs including:

1. Find news sources online or in a weekly magazine format:
There are many different news sources available, including television, radio, newspapers, and online news websites. It's a fun way to keep on top of current affairs.

2. Discuss current affairs with an adult:
Talk about news stories and discuss your opinions and thoughts about the news. Can you have a discussion with an adult about the story and do you have the same views?

3. Watch or listen to the news together with friends or family:
Watch or listen to the news together as a family and discuss the stories together. This can be a great way to practise your critical thinking skills.

4. Find news stories that interest you:
Look for news stories that relate to your interests, such as sports, science, or music. This can help make the news more relevant and engaging to you.

5. Keep a news journal:
Keep a news journal where you write about the news stories that interest you. It's a great way to remember these stories.

Here are a few example questions relating to current affairs that you might be asked in an interview.

1. What story in the news in the past few months has really caught your attention and why?

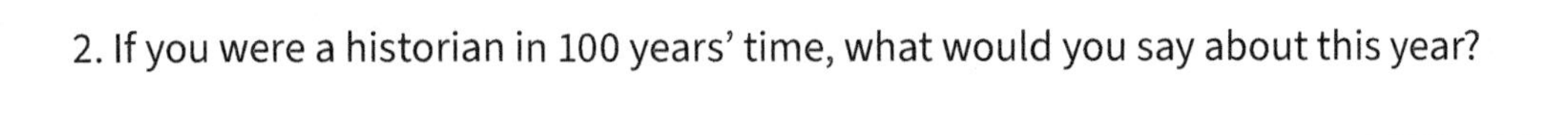

2. If you were a historian in 100 years' time, what would you say about this year?

3. What do you think UK politicians of today should prioritise?

Task: Use the templates below to **write down three news stories** you think are important or that you find interesting.

Bright Light EDUCATION

NEWSPAPER

STORY NO.01 | **THE BEST SELLING NEWSPAPER IN THE WORLD** | **Todays's Edition**

Key event:

What happened?

When did it happen?

Where did it happen?

What's your opinion on the story?

NEWSPAPER

STORY NO.02 | THE BEST SELLING NEWSPAPER IN THE WORLD | Todays's Edition

Key event:

What happened?

When did it happen?

Where did it happen?

What's your opinion on the story?

Bright Light
EDUCATION

NEWSPAPER

STORY NO.03

THE BEST SELLING NEWSPAPER IN THE WORLD

Todays's Edition

Key event:

What happened?

When did it happen?

Where did it happen?

What's your opinion on the story?

Puzzles and word games

You may be asked to solve some word puzzles, riddles or other challenges. By presenting you with these, the interviewer wants to assess your ability to think critically, logically and creatively. Remember when faced with these sorts of challenge during an interview, it's important to approach them calmly and methodically. Take your time to understand the challenge and consider different strategies for finding a solution. Explain your thought process to the interviewer, showcasing your problem-solving abilities and your ability to communicate reasoning effectively.

Brain teaser

Can you work out a word or phrase based on what you can see?

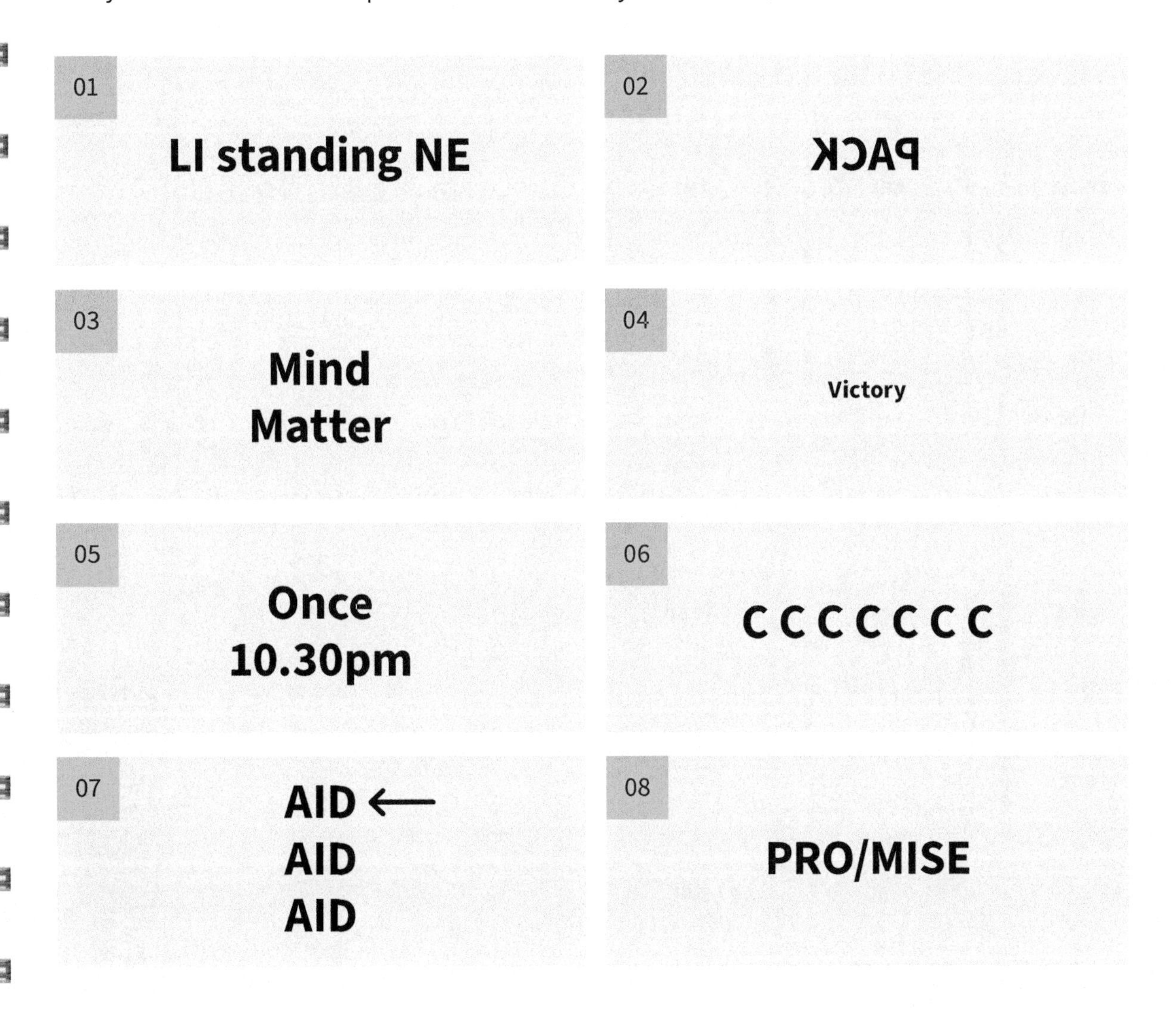

1. Standing in line **2.** Backpack **3.** Mind over matter **4.** Small victory **5.** Once upon a time **6.** The seven seas
7. First aid **8.** Broken promise

Word ladder

The interviewer selects a starting word and an ending word that are both four or five letters long (for example, "shop" and "flop"). The challenge is to create a word ladder by changing one letter at a time, with each intermediate word being a valid English word.

Task: The goal is to create the shortest word ladder possible. See example, of a possible word ladder for "shop" to "flop".

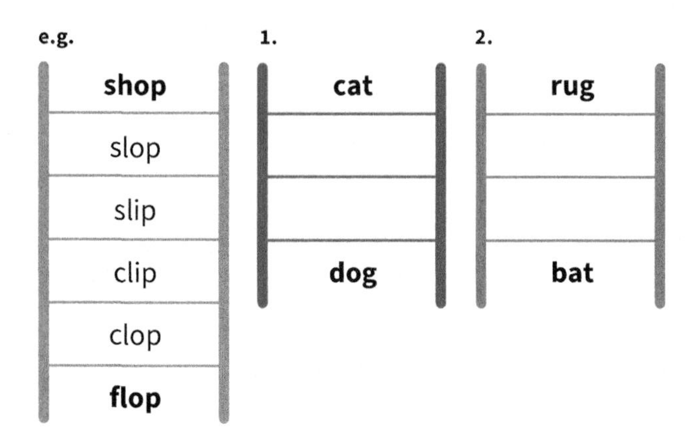

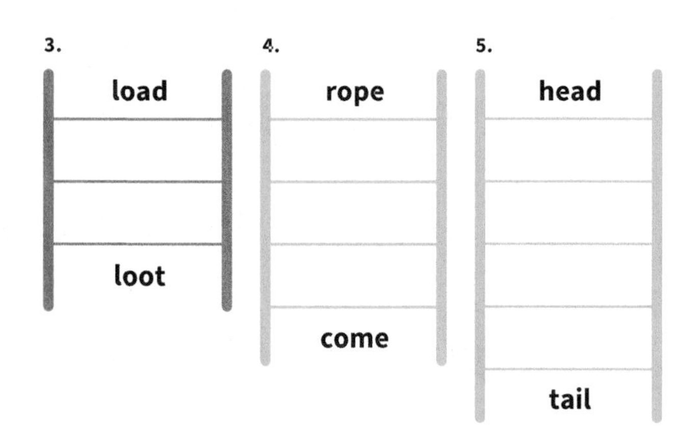

Missing letters

The interviewer provides a list of words with missing letters.

Task: The challenge is to fill in the missing letters to create the correct words. Have a go!

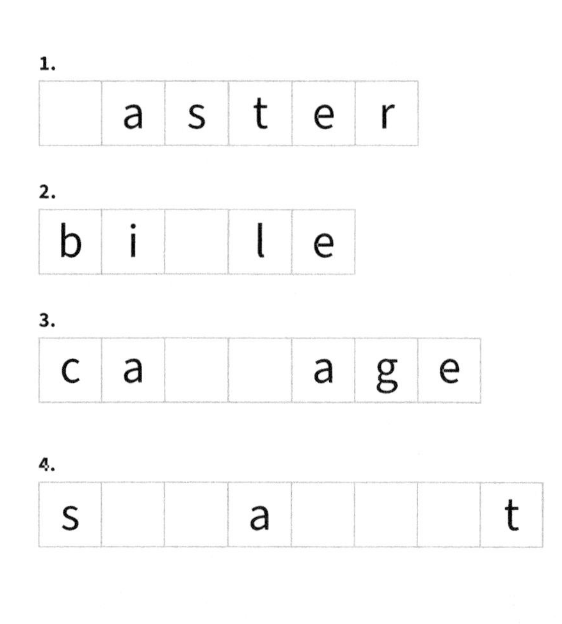

Word Ladder: 1. Cat / Cot / Dot / Dog **2.** Rug / Bug / Bag / Bat
3. Load / Loud / Lout / Loot **4.** Rope / Hope / Home / Some / Come
5. Head / Heal / Teal / Tell / Tall / Tail

Missing Letters: 1. Master **2.** Bible **3.** Cabbage **4.** Straight

Your questions

Do YOU have any questions?
Often interviewers will end an interview asking whether you have any questions. Here are some dos and don'ts to help!

DO

- Ask a question that genuinely interests you. Choosing to ask something that you are not interested in just because you want to ask an original question might get you in a tricky situation when the interviewer is an expert in the topic of your question!
- Prepare two or three questions before you go.
- Research the school and choose a question that shows you have done so. This will, in turn, show that you are eager to attend the school and want to get involved with what the school offers.
- Choose a unique question as this will make you stand out from the rest of the candidates.
- Elaborate on your question and preface it with any information about you that the interviewer might be interested in.

DON'T

- Ask a rude or mischievous question to attempt to make the interviewer laugh. It won't do you any favours and may just cross you off their list even if the rest of the interview went well!
- Ask a dull question about what time school starts. You are trying to shine and stand out in the interview and this may well just send your interviewer to sleep!
- Ask an irrelevant question for the sake of asking a question. The interviewer will see right through this!

Example questions:

- I love playing chess and have been part of the chess team at my school. I was just wondering what the opportunities for me to continue chess would be at your school?
- I organised a cake sale at my school and we raised money for WWF as I'm passionate about protecting our wildlife. Does your school run charity events and would there be opportunities for me to help with running these?
- What qualities do you believe are most important for a student to succeed at this school?

Write down 5 questions you could ask about the schools where you have interviews. Relate them to the school in question where applicable.

Sample mock interviews

Mock Interviews

A great way to prepare for your interview, is to have a mock interview. At Bright Light Education, we offer mock interviews with specialist interview teachers. After the interview, you will receive detailed feedback on your mock interview so, when the time comes, you can feel confident going into the real interview.

Task: Use the below mock interviews to help you prepare even further. Think about how you would answer each of the questions.

Sample Mock Interview 1:

1. What subject do you enjoy studying the most and why?
2. Can you give an example of a project you completed in one of your favourite subjects?
3. What hobbies or extracurricular activities do you participate in?
4. Have you ever faced any challenges in your extracurriculars? How did you overcome them?
5. How do you like to learn new things? Do you prefer hands-on activities or reading about a topic?
6. Can you give an example of something you learned recently?
7. Can you tell me about a book you read recently?
8. What did you like about the book?
9. Can you summarise the plot or main themes of the book?
10. What are some goals you have for yourself in the future?
11. Look at the image below. Can you tell me about it?

12. Answer the following maths questions:
    - If you used 3 eggs from two dozen, how many eggs do you have left?
    - What is the probability of picking a king from a pack of playing cards?
    - Jack earns £125 per day. How much does he earn in 12 days?

Sample Mock Interview 2:

1. What is one of your academic strengths?
2. What do you think sets you apart from other students applying for this school?
3. How do you handle challenging or difficult tasks?
4. What extracurricular activities are you involved in and why do you enjoy them?
5. What do you hope to achieve during your time at our school?
6. Is there a news story that has caught your attention recently? Can you tell me about it?
7. If you could create a new subject to be taught in school, what would it be and why would you introduce it?
8. You have been asked to rename the days of the week. What would you name them and why?
9. What book are you reading at the moment? Can you tell me a bit about it?
10. I have a riddle for you to try and solve:
    I am taken from a mine and shut up in a wooden case, from which I am never released.
    I am used by almost every student.

    What am I?
11. Read the text below:

    There was an Old Man with a beard,
    Who said, "It is just as I feared! -
    Two Owls and a Hen,
    Four Larks and a Wren,
    Have all built their nests in my beard!"
    By Edward Lear

    What can you tell me about this text?
12. Do you have any questions for me?

Sample answers to interview questions

About You and Your Family

What activities do you like to do with your family?
This is a simple question not trying to trick you out, but trying to find out more about what you like to do!

For example:
"We organise game nights which I love. We have a massive collection of board games and card games that we play together. We're all quite competitive so it can get quite heated! It's really fun though and we always end up laughing our heads off, especially when we play 'Articulate'!"

Tell me about a book you have read. Why did you like it? What would you change about it?
This is a common question so make sure you have a good, honest, clear answer! Choose a book that you have loved and that you can speak confidently about.

For example:
"One of my favourite books that I've read recently is "The Hunger Games" by Suzanne Collins. I loved this book because it was really exciting and kept me on the edge of my seat the whole time! One thing I really liked about the book was the strong and brave main character, Katniss Everdeen. She's such a good role model. I thought it was amazing how she stood up for what she believed in. If I could change one thing about the book, it would be to include more details about the history of Panem and how the Hunger Games came to be. I think this would have added more depth to the story and made it even more interesting."

Tell me about a real interest you have, either in or out of school.
This is a perfect opportunity to discuss something that really interests you and will make you stand out from others. Show enthusiasm and motivation towards this interest of yours; be genuine and passionate about your answer.

For example:
"One of my biggest interests is playing the piano. I've been taking lessons for several years now and I really enjoy it. I love the feeling of being able to express myself through music and the sense of accomplishment when I master a new piece. It's also a great way for me to relax and de-stress after a busy day at school. In fact, I've even started composing my own music, which has been a really fun challenge."

What is your greatest strength?
It's important to give an honest and thoughtful answer that demonstrates self-awareness and a positive attitude. Speak confidently but also be humble and avoid any bragging!

For example:
"I'd say one of my biggest strengths is my determination. I'm very determined when it comes to completing something! When I set my mind to something, I have to make sure I achieve it and my mum even says I can be very stubborn with it too as I won't concentrate on anything else until it's completed!"

What three words would you use to describe yourself?
Here, choose words that accurately reflect your personality, strengths, and values.

For example:
"I would describe myself as curious, determined, and empathetic. I'm always asking questions and wanting to learn new things and, when I set my mind to something, I work hard to achieve it and don't give up easily. And I've been told I'm empathetic too."

What do you want to be when you grow up?
Be honest and enthusiastic about your answer, while also acknowledging that your goals may change over time.

For example:
"Right now, I'm really interested in becoming a vet. I've always loved animals and I think it would be a really fulfilling and rewarding job. I love learning about different animal species and how they behave. My dad told me he always wanted to be a vet when he grew up and then now he's a lawyer so I know that I might change my mind as I get older! At the moment though, I'd like to be a vet!"

If you had 2 hours of free time, what would you do?
This is a great time to demonstrate any interests and values.

For example:
"If I had two hours of free time, I would probably go on a bike ride with my dad. I just got a new bike and we went out to Richmond Park and had hot chocolate after. It was a really nice way to spend the afternoon. If it was raining though then I'd probably read my new Beano magazine – I love comic books!"

Sample answers to interview questions

Tell me about something you found difficult and what happened.
With this sort of question, be honest and focus on how you overcame the challenge.

For example:
"One thing that I found difficult was learning a new instrument. I had always been interested in music, but when I started playing the guitar, I found it difficult to coordinate my fingers – I kept getting in such a muddle! I felt pretty frustrated to begin with, but I kept going and practiced lots, even when I didn't feel like practising, and I started to get better and enjoy playing more. Now I can play lots of songs and I even performed in the Year 6 concert last week which I enjoyed."

Who is your favourite sportsperson, musician or artist?
Choose someone that you genuinely admire and can speak about with enthusiasm.

For example:
"My favourite artist is Frida Kahlo. I love how she used bright colours and bold patterns to create powerful images. I also think she's a great role model for anyone who wants to be creative and express themselves in their own unique way."

If you could be anyone for a day, who would you be?
Choose someone you admire or are curious about, and be able to explain why.

For example:
"If I could be anyone for a day, I would choose to be Marcus Rashford. Not only would that mean that I could play football all day, but also I just think he's such a brilliant human being! He's used his fame to do some incredible things like helping homeless people and ensuring more children receive free school meals. Plus, I have loved reading his books too, so I'd be able to write like him for the day!"

About you and your school

What is your favourite subject and why?

Don't answer by saying that you love all subjects equally. It's not true and the interviewer won't believe you! If you'd like to choose a couple of subjects, that's fine but do settle on your favourite and explain why.

For example:

"I love maths, science and PE but if I had to pick one favourite, I'd say science. The world around me really interests me plus I love science experiments. For my birthday, I always ask for science kits!"

What is your least favourite subject and why?

This is not a time for you to say how bad you are at English or maths or how much you hate a subject! Instead, be honest, but try and make it positive in some aspect!

For example:

"My least favourite subject is maths. I find it challenging to understand some of the concepts and it takes me longer to work through problems compared to other subjects. But I do always get there in the end and I'm not afraid to ask the teacher to help me. I know how important maths is so I'm keen to become more confident in it."

What would your teachers say about you if I asked them?

Here, demonstrate that you have a positive relationship with your teachers and are well-regarded by them.

For example:

"I believe my teachers would say that I am a hardworking and dedicated pupil who always strives to do my best. I try to participate actively in class, ask questions when I don't understand something, and complete all of my work to the best of my ability. I also try to be respectful and supportive of my classmates, and I'm always willing to help out."

What extra-curricular activities do you do?

Here is your chance to showcase your interests and involvement in activities outside of school.

For example:

"I'm involved in a few different activities outside of school. One of my favourites is playing football for Barnes Eagles. I love playing football and I've met some of my best friends outside school. I'm also part of a robotics club where we work on building and programming robots. It's really fun but also pretty tricky at times and I've learned so much about programming. Those are my two favourites!"

Sample answers to interview questions

Tell me about a piece of group work or teamwork you were involved in.
With this sort of question, highlight your teamwork skills and give an example of how you successfully collaborated with others.

For example:
"One example of a piece of group work I was involved in was a science project where we had to build a model of the solar system. Our group of four had to research the planets, figure out how to create an accurate scale model, and then present our project to the class. We all had different strengths and interests, so we divided up the tasks according to what we were best at. For example, I focused on the research and writing the presentation script while one of my teammates was in charge of the design and construction of the model. We all worked together to make sure that everything came together on time and that we were all prepared for the presentation. We were all really proud of what we had created as a team."

What would your dream school be like?
This question is asking you what your interests and priorities are when it comes to education.

For example:
"My dream school would be a place where learning is enjoyable but also challenging. I would want teachers who are passionate about what they teach. I would also want a school that offers lots of extracurricular activities. I love all the clubs I do before and after school, so I think these are an important part of a school. Finally, it's vital that the school has a good sense of community where everyone feels included and supported. A bit like having a big family!"

Do you have a school responsibility? What have you learned from this role?
Here, highlight your experiences and the skills you have gained through your school responsibilities.

For example:
"Yes, I'm a prefect at my school. We have to look out for good behaviour from other children and we're allowed to give out behaviour points. We also meet with the Headteacher once every half-term to discuss ways to improve our school. I've loved having the responsibility and it's been lovely helping with the younger children. We also have to speak to prospective parents too and that's been good for building my confidence."

What would you change about your school?
It's important to approach this question thoughtfully and constructively! It will show the interviewer what matters to you. Try and keep it as positive as possible!

For example:
"I would change some of the after-school clubs on offer. Don't get me wrong, some are brilliant and I go to art club and cricket club. I just wish they changed them each term so that we could try new and different skills. I heard of a school that did a dissection club once which sounds brilliant. Also, my cousin has bee-keeping club – that would be amazing!"

About this school

What attracts you to our school?
It's important to show that you have done your research on the school and can highlight specific aspects that appeal to you.

For example:
"One thing that particularly attracts me is the strong sense of community that I have heard about. I think it's important to feel like you are part of a supportive and welcoming place when you're at school, and I get the sense that your school is like that. I'm interested in sports and music, and I have seen that you have lots of opportunities for these. I'd love to become part of the football team and orchestra if I can!"

What will you contribute to this school?
Show that you are enthusiastic about making a positive impact in the school community.

For example:
"I believe that I can make a positive contribution to this school in a number of ways. Firstly, I am passionate about learning and I always strive to do my best academically. I believe that my dedication and hard work will be an asset to the school. Also, I am heavily involved in extracurricular activities such as sports and music, and I am excited about the opportunity to represent the school in music competitions and sports matches. Finally, I am a friendly and approachable person, and I believe that I can contribute to the school community by being a positive and supportive presence for my fellow students."

Is there anything about this school which would be challenging for you?
It's important to be honest and upfront about any potential challenges, while also showing that you are willing to put in the effort to overcome them.

For example:
"I'm excited about the prospect of attending this school, and I believe that it would be a great fit for me. However, I think it will take me a little time to adjust to the new environment and making new friends. The school I currently go to is pretty small and being in year 6, I'm one of the oldest. Coming to this school will be a bit of a shock! I'm keen to get involved in extracurricular activities though so I think this will help me settle in more quickly."

Which other schools have you applied to? Which one is your favourite?
Here, it's important to be honest while also showing that you are genuinely interested in the school you are interviewing for.

For example:
"I have applied to several schools as I am eager to find the best fit for me. However, this school is my top choice because of [insert reasons why you like the school here]."

Complex ideas

What makes a good teacher?
Here it is important to show that you have given some thought to what qualities are important in an effective teacher.

For example:
"I think a good teacher is someone who is knowledgeable about their subject and also passionate about teaching it. I think you can really tell when a teacher loves what they teach and, if they do, it transfers straight to their students."

What makes a good pupil?
It's important to show that you have an understanding of what qualities are important for being successful in school.

For example:
"In my opinion, a good pupil is someone who is motivated, responsible, and respectful. They should be motivated to learn and also willing to put in the effort. I think it's also important that they are respectful towards their teachers and friends."

If you could have any job for a day, what would it be and why?
Show your passions and interests in this answer!

For example:
"If I could have any job for a day, I would choose to be an astronaut. I have always been fascinated by space and the idea of exploring the unknown. Being able to experience weightlessness and see the Earth from space would be an incredible adventure."

If you were given £300, what would you do with it and why?
Think about an original answer for this and be honest!

For example:
"If I were given £300, I would save part of it. I would then use some of it to buy myself a new tennis racquet (mine is really old and the handle is falling apart!). I would also donate some of it to the RSPCA as I love animals and it's a charity I've raised money for before and it's important to me. If I had any left over, then I would buy my brother a book he is desperate for!"

If you were a superhero, what would your superpower be?
Being original here will make your answer stand out from the rest and be memorable to the interviewer.

For example:
"If I were a superhero, I would want my superpower to be the ability to fly. I think being able to fly would give me a sense of freedom and allow me to travel quickly and easily to different places, whether it's to help someone in need or to explore new parts of the world. Plus, flying would be really fun!"

If you could solve one problem in the world, what would it be and why?
Let your originality and honesty shine through again here!

For example:
"If I could solve one problem in the world, I would want to solve the problem of climate change. It's a global issue that affects everyone so if I could solve this problem, then it would be beneficial to so many people and future generations. It upsets me to think of the damage climate change is causing to our world so it would be a definite problem to fix!

Describe a future invention and how it would affect our lives.
This could be anything at all so it's worth researching something that you are interested in yourself.

For example:
"One future invention that I find fascinating is driverless cars. I find it amazing that these cars would have the ability to drive themselves. They would benefit people who are unable to drive themselves, such as the elderly or disabled. And these cars would be designed to be more environmentally friendly, reducing emissions and helping to stop the effects of climate change."

What do you think has been the best scientific invention?
There is no wrong answer to this, but worth preparing for a similar question so that you are confident in speaking about an important scientific invention.

For example:
"I think that the best scientific invention has been the Internet. The Internet has transformed the way we live, work and communicate with people. It has made information accessible to people all over the world and has allowed people to connect with others regardless of where they live. It has definitely had a profound impact on our lives, and has made the world a more accessible place."

What period of time would you like to go back to and why?
Be honest in your answer and choose a time that you genuinely find interesting and know something about.

For example:
"I love art so I would love to go back to the Renaissance period. It was a time of great creativity and innovation, where many of the world's greatest artists and thinkers were producing their most iconic works. I think it would be fascinating to see how people lived during this time, and to witness some of the amazing breakthroughs that were being made in art. Plus, I would love to see some of the famous works of art that were created during this period, like Leonardo da Vinci's 'Mona Lisa' – it's my favourite painting!"

If you could meet any person in the world, either dead or alive, who would it be and why?
Remember to elaborate on your answer and provide reasons for your choice, as well as showing enthusiasm and interest in the person you would like to meet.

For example:
"I would love to meet my grandmother. She died before I was born and I've heard so much about her from my mum, but I wish I could meet her. I'd ask her whether my mum was naughty when she was a child!"

Tell me something you have taught yourself.
Speak confidently about your taught skill and remember it can be anything at all! Think outside of the box to ensure your answer stands out from others. For example,

"I taught myself how to solve the Rubik's Cube! I got one for Christmas last year and was determined to work out how to do it, so I bought a book on solving them and learned from there. Now I'm trying to get quicker each time!"

Unusual questions

Think of as many things as possible that you could do with a pen other than use it as a pen.
A perfect example of a question you cannot predict! There is no right or wrong answer, just make sure you back up your answer with well-thought out reasons.

For example:
"There are lots of things that you could do with a pen. You could use it as a screwdriver, particularly for small screws. You could use it as a drumstick or to create sound effects in music. Pens can also be used for fidgeting or stress relief, as they can be spun, twirled, or flipped between your fingers."

This watch doesn't have batteries. How do the hands move?
A question that has come up in a past interview, but unlikely to come up again!
Worthwhile thinking how you might answer a question like this one though.

For example:
"Inside the watch, there are gears and springs that work together to make the watch work. When the spring is wound, it creates energy. As the spring unwinds, the gears and hands move. Of course, now most people have smart watches that don't use the gears and springs!"

What would you do with a brick?
Another wonderfully unusual question! The interviewer is looking for creativity in your answer.

For example:
"There are actually quite a few things that you can do with a brick! You could use it as a doorstop or a paperweight, or even as a bookend. You could also use it as a weight to hold down a tent, or as a tool to help break up hard soil or rocks in a garden. If you were feeling creative, you could even use it as a base for a DIY birdhouse."

If you were given the ability to talk to animals for one day, how would you use this unique opportunity?

"This would be amazing! If I was given this ability, I would consider it a perfect chance to spend time in natural environments, such as forests, oceans, or parks, engaging in conversations with various animals. I would listen carefully to their perspectives, and gain a deeper understanding of their behaviours and habitats."

How many ice-cubes would fill this room?

This is a classic example of an open-ended problem that does not have a straightforward answer. The most important thing is for the interviewer to hear your thought process. Will you make a wild guess or will you try and do a calculation?

For example:

"I would have to measure the length, width and height of this room to find the volume of the room. Then I would need to find the volume of an ice cube and work out how many would fit into the volume of the room."

How does a radio work?

If you're not sure of the answer to this sort of question, then be honest with the interviewer and explain that you're not sure, but that you would like to have a guess! If you do know, then give as much detail as possible.

For example:

"A radio operates by receiving radio waves, which are transmitted through the air from a broadcasting station. The radio's antenna picks up these waves and sends them to the tuner, which selects the desired frequency. The tuner then sends this signal to the radio's amplifier, which increases the strength of the signal, and sends it to the radio's speaker, which converts the electrical signal into sound waves that we can hear."

Tell me something about this banana.

Another obscure question where the interviewer is looking for an interesting and creative answer! Feel free to have some fun with it too!

"Way to make me hungry! This banana is a piece of fruit that grows on a banana tree. It is usually yellow in colour and has a slightly curved shape. Bananas are a good source of potassium and other vitamins and minerals, making them a healthy snack. They can be eaten on their own or used in recipes such as banana bread, smoothies, or even ice cream. This particular banana looks ripe and ready to eat, with no brown spots or bruises. Overall, it seems like a tasty snack option."

Higher order questions

How should we be supporting people who have no home?
Here, the interviewer is looking for some analysis from you. There is no right answer so use it as an opportunity to discuss the issue.

For example:
"Personally, I think that while it's important to be compassionate and help those in need, giving money directly to people living on the street may not always be the best solution. Instead, supporting local charities and organisations that work with people experiencing homelessness can be a more effective way to make a difference in their lives. These organisations can provide shelter, food, and support services to help these people get back on their feet and improve their situation in the long term."

Is there more happiness or unhappiness in the world?
Show the interviewer that you're interested in discussing complex ideas like this.

For example:
"This is a difficult question to answer because happiness and unhappiness are subjective experiences that can vary greatly from person to person. There are certainly many sources of unhappiness in the world, such as poverty, conflict, illness, and inequality. These are all very real problems that can cause a great deal of suffering. However, there are also many sources of happiness in the world, such as love, friendship, creativity, and achievement. Many people are able to find happiness even in difficult circumstances, and there are many examples of people who have overcome real difficulties to live happy lives."

What colour would a zebra be if it lost all its stripes?
Sometimes an interviewer will spring a complex question like this one on you to see how you react and how you go about answering it!

For example:
"A zebra probably wouldn't survive long if it lost its stripes as they rely on their stripes for camouflage and protection from predators! But, hypothetically, it would be a black animal because the colour of a zebra's skin is black. The white stripes are created because there are certain areas where there is no pigment."

Is it possible to have a box with nothing inside?
Another question where the interviewer is looking for your problem solving style thinking!

For example:
"I would say it's possible to have a box with nothing inside as it can be completely empty, without any objects inside. However, even an empty box contains air molecules, so the space inside the box is not truly empty as it is filled with air!"

Should billions of pounds be spent on space exploration when there is poverty in the world?
Show your understanding of both sides to the argument, but feel free to choose one side as a conclusion if you like.

For example:
"On the one hand, space exploration has the potential to lead to important scientific discoveries and technological advancements that could benefit humanity. However, the billions of pounds spent on it could be better used to address things such as poverty, hunger, and inequality. These issues affect millions of people around the world. I think I'd like to see some of the money used to address these."

Should we all become vegan to reduce carbon emissions and habitat destruction caused by meat production?
This is another debate style question where you need to show an understanding of both sides of the argument.

For example:
"I do think meat production does significantly contribute to greenhouse gas emissions. Switching to a vegan diet, or at least reducing meat consumption, can help to reduce these negative environmental impacts. However, reducing meat consumption isn't the only solution to reducing carbon emissions and habitat destruction. There are other actions that can be made, such as promoting renewable energy, reducing air travel, supporting sustainable agriculture, and reducing waste. We can all help in different ways."

The police want greater access to the public's personal data (e.g. Internet search history, encrypted phone messages). What's more important, your right to personal privacy or public safety?
Looking at both sides of the argument here is important even if you believe strongly for one side.

For example:
"I believe there needs to be a balance between personal privacy and public safety. If you allow greater access to personal data by the police while it may help to prevent some crimes and improve public safety, it could also lead to the abuse of personal data. Also, there is a risk that the data could be used in ways that are discriminatory or biased against certain groups. However, greater access to personal data by the police could help to identify and prevent crimes before they occur, and it could help to apprehend criminals."

The voting age in England is 18 (in general elections), but there are discussions about changing it. What do you think the voting age should be and why?
There is no right answer to this and if you feel strongly for one side of the argument, then it's important to show this in your answer. It's also important though to show that you appreciate the other side of the argument.

For example:
"On the one hand, some argue that lowering the voting age to 16 would encourage young people to become more involved in politics. It could also help to ensure that young people have a say in decisions that will affect their futures. On the other hand, some argue that 16-year-olds may not yet have the necessary life experience or maturity to make sensible political decisions. In my opinion, I think keeping it at 18 is the right thing to do."

Mental maths

If a car travels 100 miles in 2 hours, what is its average speed per hour?
To find the average speed per hour, you need to divide the total distance travelled by the total time taken.
- Average speed = total distance ÷ total time
- In this case, the car travelled 100 miles in 2 hours.
- Average speed = 100 miles ÷ 2 hours = 50 miles per hour
- Therefore, the car's average speed per hour was **50 miles per hour**

What is a third of three quarters of 1000?
To find a third of three quarters of 1000, you can follow these steps:
- Find three quarters of 1000 by multiplying 1000 by 0.75: 1000 x 0.75 = 750
- Find one third of 750 by dividing 750 by 3: 750 ÷ 3 = 250
- Therefore, a third of three quarters of 1000 is **250**

How many faces does a hexagonal based prism have?
A hexagonal based prism has a total of 8 faces – 2 hexagonal bases and 6 rectangular faces.

What is 20% of 600?
- Work out what 10% is by dividing 600 by 10 = 60
- Then multiple 60 by 2 to find 20% = **120**

What is the percentage increase from 20 to 30?
- Find out the difference between the two numbers: 10
- Divide the increase by the original number and multiply the answer by 100: (10 ÷ 20) x 100 = **50%**

A rectangle has a length of 18 cm and a width of 9 cm.
What is the area of the rectangle?
To find the area of a rectangle, you can multiply its length by its width.
In this case, the length is 18 cm and the width is 9 cm.
- Area of rectangle = length x width
- Area of rectangle = 18 cm x 9 cm
- Area of rectangle = **162 square cm**

A store sells 25 bags of rice each day. If each bag contains 2.5 kg of rice, how many kg of rice are sold in one week (7 days)?
- 25 bags/day x 7 days/week = 175 bags/week
- Since each bag contains 2.5 kg of rice, the store sells in one week:
- 175 bags/week x 2.5 kg/bag = 437.5 kg/week
- Therefore, the store sells **437.5 kg** of rice in one week (7 days).

Calculate 2896 + 384
To calculate this mentally, one method is to:
- Add the hundreds first: 2896 + 300 = 3196
- Then add the tens: 3196 + 80 = 3276
- Then add the units: 3276 + 4 = **3280**

Work out 241 ÷ 25
We know that 25 goes into 100 4 times
- so therefore it will go 8 times into 200.
- 25 goes into 41 once with a remainder of 16
- so your answer is 9 remainder **16**.

Which two numbers have a sum of 15 and a product of 36?
The easiest way to work this out is think of the factors of 36:
- 1 and 36
- 2 and 18
- 3 and 12
- 4 and 9
- 6 and 6

Of these factors, 3 and 12 make **15** so this is your answer.

Check out our other Bright Light books!

Bright Light Phonics Series

Book 1 | Phase 2   Book 2 | Phase 3   Book 3 | Phase 4

Phonics Activity Books for 3-5 year olds

The Bright Light Phonics books are ideal for preschool, Reception and Year 1 children as well as those children who are homeschooled. Written by two experienced primary school teachers and mothers, these phonics workbooks introduce children to new sounds and allow them the opportunity to read and write with growing confidence.

A note from the authors: *"Watching your child learn to read and write can be a wonderfully exciting time! As mothers ourselves, we have seen first-hand the joy children get from being able to recognise their first sounds, words and sentences. Structured in a weekly format, we hope our workbooks will provide a straightforward and enjoyable way in which to guide your child on their phonics journey!"*

Creative Writing Skills

Supporting Creative Writing for ages 7–14

This inspiring combination of teaching guide and activity workbook, in an easily accessible format, will help children to produce compelling stories. It is perfect for 7–14 year olds, including children sitting entrance examinations, those who are home-schooled, or those who simply wish to improve their story writing.

"Great tool for 11+ exam prep! Creative writing is so difficult to teach for a parent. We really struggled until we discovered this book. It provides an easy structured approach with engaging activities. We've seen a marked improvement in my daughter's writing. Definitely recommend!" – Parent

All editions available to buy from Amazon.